Garfield County Libraries
Gordon Cooper Branch Library
76 South 4th Street
Carbondale, CO 81623
(970) 963-2889 Fax (970) 963-8573
www.garfieldlibraries.org

# Cinco de Mayo

**ABDO**
Publishing Company

A Buddy Book
by
Julie Murray

Visit us at
www.abdopub.com

Published by ABDO Publishing Company, 4940 Viking Drive, Edina, Minnesota 55435.

Edited by: Sarah Tieck
Contributing Editor: Michael P. Goecke
Graphic Design: Denise Esner
Image Research: Deborah Coldiron, Maria Hosley
Photographs: BrandX, Corbis, Digital Vision, Flat Earth, Hulton Archives, Image Ideas, Photodisc

## Library of Congress Cataloging-in-Publication Data

Murray, Julie, 1969-
   Cinco de Mayo / Julie Murray.
      p. cm. — (Holidays)
   Includes bibliographical references.
   ISBN 1-59197-586-7 (alk. paper)
      1. Cinco de Mayo (Mexican holiday)—Juvenile literature. 2. Mexico—Social life and customs—Juvenile literature. 3. Cinco de Mayo, Battle of, Puebla, Mexico, 1862—Juvenile literature. [1. Cinco de Mayo (Mexican holiday). 2. Holidays. 3. Mexico—Social life and customs.] I. Title.

F1233.M975 2005
394.262—dc22

                                                                          2003065512

# Table of Contents

# What Is Cinco de Mayo?

Cinco de Mayo is a national holiday in Mexico. It happens on May 5 each year. Cinco de Mayo is Spanish for "the fifth of May." This is the date Mexico won a great battle in 1862. People celebrate this day with parades, food, music, and dancing.

The flag of Mexico.

# Mexico At A Glance

**Location:** North America

**Borders:** United States, Guatemala, Belize, Pacific Ocean, Gulf of Mexico

**Capital:** Mexico City

**Population:** 103 million people

**Size:** 756,066 square miles (1,958,201 sq km)

**Official Language:** Spanish

**Flag:** Red, white, and green stripes

**Money:** Pesos

**Number of States:** 31

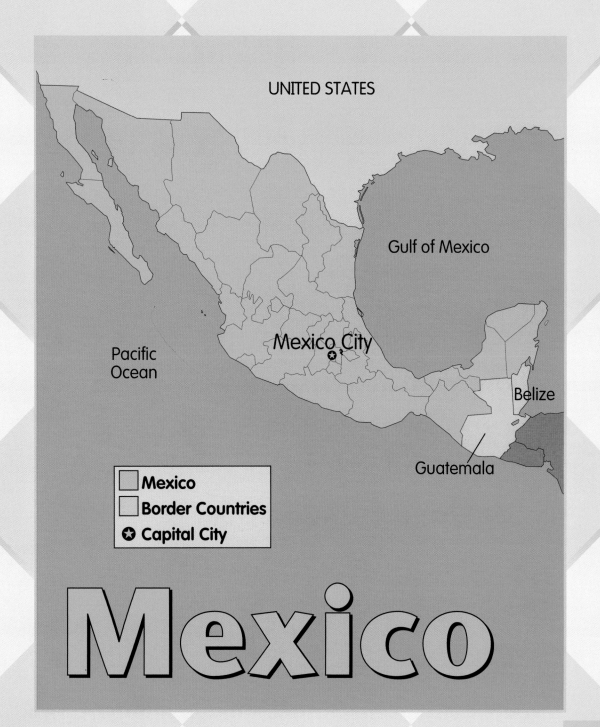

UNITED STATES

Gulf of Mexico

Pacific
Ocean

Mexico City ⭐

Belize

Guatemala

- ☐ Mexico
- ☐ Border Countries
- ⭐ Capital City

# Mexico

# The Battle Of Puebla

May 5, 1862, is important in Mexico's history. The Battle of Puebla happened that day. The Mexican people fought against French soldiers and won. This battle made Mexico stronger.

Napoleon III was the ruler of France during the war with Mexico.

In 1862, Mexico and France were fighting a war. The war started because Mexico owed money to France. Mexico did not have the money to pay them. France wanted to take over Mexico. Mexico was a weak country. It had a small army.

On May 5, 1862, the French army came to the town of Puebla. Puebla is near Mexico City. The president of Mexico told the army to defend Puebla. People came from nearby villages to help. Many lives were in danger.

The people and soldiers fought hard. After a few hours the French retreated. This was an important battle in the war for Mexico's independence. Mexico won this war in 1867.

# Cinco de Mayo Traditions

For many, Cinco de Mayo begins with remembering the Battle of Puebla. This is a Cinco de Mayo custom. People dress in soldier uniforms. Then they pretend to fight the battle between Mexico and France. When Mexico wins, people shout *"Viva Mexico!"* This is Spanish for "Long live Mexico!"

Piñatas are often made in the shapes of animals.

After that, it is time for a fiesta. Fiesta is a Spanish word that means "party." Children play Loteria, which is like bingo. They also take turns hitting the piñata. When the piñata breaks, candy spills out. Cinco de Mayo also includes parades, food, music, and dancing.

# Mexican Foods

Food is part of Cinco de Mayo. Tacos and burritos are Mexican foods. So are beans, tamales, and salsa. Menudo is a traditional soup eaten on Cinco de Mayo. It is spicy. The cooks make it using chili peppers and spices.

Traditional Mexican foods are served for Cinco de Mayo.

Tortillas are another favorite food. These are made with corn or flour. People use them to hold meat, vegetables, and cheese. Tortillas can be fried into hard shells for chips or tacos. Sometimes they are baked for burritos and enchiladas.

Tacos are tortilla shells filled with meat, cheese, and vegetables.

# Musical Traditions

Mariachi bands play traditional Mexican music at fiestas. Mariachi means "musician." Band members play guitars, trumpets, violins, maracas, and other instruments. They dress in black suits, like Mexican cowboys.

Maracas are sometimes decorated with the colors of Mexico's flag.

15

The songs mariachis play are called corridos. Corridos is a Spanish word for songs that tell stories. Many of these songs are very old.  The words often tell stories of the past.

Mariachi band members dress like Mexican cowboys.

# Mexican Dancers

Dancing is a part of Mexico's culture, too. The most popular dance is the Mexican hat dance. It is the national dance of Mexico. During this dance, a Mexican hat called a sombrero is put on the ground. The dancers move around the hat and stomp their heels on the ground.

Sombreros are one part of colorful Mexican costumes.

Mexican dancers wear colorful costumes. There are different costumes for different dances. The women wear skirts with ruffles. They twirl the skirt while they dance.

The men wear sombreros and short black jackets. Their pants have silver buttons down the sides. They also wear colorful scarves around their waists.

# Cinco de Mayo In America

There are celebrations in the United States, too. Cinco de Mayo is not an official holiday in the United States. Still, there have been celebrations in the United States for about 100 years. Many Americans came from Mexico.

Dancing is a part
of Cinco de Mayo.

There are many activities on Cinco de Mayo. People in the United States have parades, carnivals, special foods, and fireworks. Cinco de Mayo is a day that many people celebrate Mexico's freedom.

Music is part of many Cinco de Mayo celebrations.

# Important Words

culture   the customs of a group of people.

custom   a practice that has been around a
   long time.

fiesta   Spanish word for party.

holiday   a special time for celebration.

retreat   to back away.

sombrero   a large-brimmed hat worn in Mexico.

# Web Sites

**To learn more about Cinco de Mayo,**
visit ABDO Publishing Company on the World Wide Web.
Web site links about Cinco de Mayo are featured on our
Book Links page. These links are routinely monitored and
updated to provide the most current information available.

www.abdopub.com

# Index